IMAGES
of America

AMELIA ISLAND

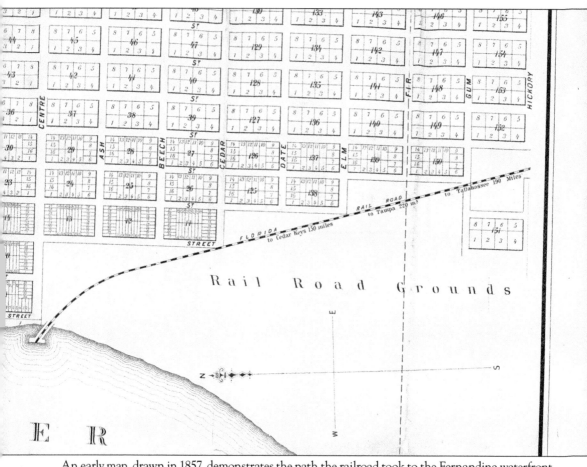

An early map, drawn in 1857, demonstrates the path the railroad took to the Fernandina waterfront. Trains loaded with lumber and other Florida resources were transported between Fernandina and Cedar Key on the Gulf Coast. The impact of the railroads resulted in robust economies for both communities. (Courtesy P. K. Yonge Library of Florida History.)

ON THE COVER: With fertile waters surrounding them, many island residents enjoyed fishing. Pictured here from left to right are Edward Williams, Capt. Robert Downes, Reverend Glass, ? Moody, Capt. Jones Davis, unidentified, Judge Rhydon Mays Call, and William Bell. A small boy also poses in the back. April 19, 1907, was a productive day for the group, who caught 42 fish, 36 of which were drum, for a total of 1,890 pounds of fish.

IMAGES
of America

AMELIA ISLAND

Rob Hicks in association with
the Amelia Island Museum of History

ARCADIA
PUBLISHING

Published by Arcadia Publishing
Charleston, South Carolina

Library of Congress Catalog Card Number: 2007923199

For all general information contact Arcadia Publishing at:
Telephone 843-853-2070
Fax 843-853-0044
E-mail sales@arcadiapublishing.com
For customer service and orders:
Toll-Free 1-888-313-2665

Visit us on the Internet at www.arcadiapublishing.com

The Amelia Island Museum of History is now housed in the county's old jail at 233 South Third Street. The building was originally constructed in 1878. In 1979, it was converted into the museum by the Duncan Lamont Clinch Historical Society. Today the museum has six employees and a host of volunteers who are dedicated to preserving the rich and unique history of Amelia Island and Fernandina Beach.

CONTENTS

ACKNOWLEDGMENTS

Many individuals and organizations made this production possible but none so much as the individuals from Fernandina's past. Without their diligence in preserving the history of this community, projects like this would not be possible. Those who have always supported the Amelia Island Museum of History also deserve credit for this endeavor. Through the donation of numerous historical artifacts, manuscripts, and photographs to the museum, Amelia's history has been preserved. A portion of the museum's photographic collection is represented by the uncredited images in this book. I would personally like to thank Rhonda Norheim for her belief in this project and her assistance in making it happen. I wish to thank the Florida State Archives and the P. K. Yonge Library of Florida History for providing some of the images used here and the Television Productions program at Fernandina Beach High School for the use of their resources in acquiring some of the images. Lastly, I'd like to thank my grandmother, grandfather, and father for their gift of writing and my wife for her unending support and patience.

An elephant parades down Centre Street with an advertisement for Allan's shoe store.

INTRODUCTION

At the northeasternmost corner of Florida lies a barrier island named Amelia. The island is small—roughly 13 miles long by 2 miles wide. It is about the size of Manhattan. However, for such a small island, it is home to a remarkably rich history. It is the only location in the United States to have had eight different flags flown over it. The first of these was raised by the French in 1562. The Spanish were always aware of the importance of amassing territories in the New World and soon seized control of Amelia, raising their own flag. They established a mission to the Timucuan Indians that lived in the area. As time passed, the island became a buffer zone between the British colony of Georgia and Spanish Florida.

After the Spanish defeat in the French and Indian War, England took possession of Florida in 1763. The British crown assigned land grants in Florida, and an indigo plantation was subsequently established on Amelia. Eventually, however, the American colonists would defeat England's primary efforts in North America. As part of the 1783 Treaty of Paris that ended the Revolutionary War, Florida was returned to Spain and their flag flew over Amelia once more.

This time, the Spanish worked to strengthen defenses on the island. They built a simple fort and platted a small town at the northern end of Amelia Island that they called Fernandina. The island again became an important border between Spanish Florida and the newly independent United States to the north. Despite the presence of the fort, the Spanish did not have the resources to keep order on Amelia or in its harbor. Because of Thomas Jefferson's Embargo Act and Spanish weakness, Amelia became the back door to the United States as pirates, smugglers, and other ne'er-do-wells used the island as a launching point to carry their goods into the United States. While the American economy struggled in its infant state, Fernandina prospered.

The War of 1812 between the United States and England eventually loomed. Pres. James Madison, leery of a British takeover of the weaker Spanish Florida, devised a plan with Gen. George Mathews wherein the residents of Florida would themselves revolt against the Spanish and give their newly conquered land to the United States. This would allow the United States to seize east Florida without directly attacking Spanish land. The group selected to lead the rebellion called itself the Patriots of Florida. On March 17, 1812, the Patriots moved towards the Spanish fort on Amelia Island. The many American gunboats in the area incorrectly led the Spanish soldiers to believe that the boats were ready to fire on the fort, and they surrendered without a shot. Yet, the boats had specific orders not to aid in the rebellion. Regardless, the Patriots were able to occupy Amelia and raised their own flag. One day later, the Patriots presented Amelia Island to the United States and the American flag was raised. However, within several weeks, the Spanish caught wind of the United States' role in the whole affair and demanded retribution. Hoping to avoid international rancor, Madison returned Amelia to the Spanish.

The Spanish soon built a stronger fort named San Carlos on Amelia but still did not have the resources needed to truly protect the island from conquest. In 1817, a Scotsman named Gregor MacGregor, who was nothing short of one of world history's most successful con men, gathered a small group of men in Darien, Georgia, with his eye on Amelia. He sent a scout to Fernandina with a rumor that he had an army of 1,000 men poised to invade the island. MacGregor clearly was a successful fraud because on June 29, Fort San Carlos was surrendered to MacGregor and a mere 55 other men after only one shot was fired. MacGregor raised the Green Cross of Florida over the island. He intended to run Amelia as a sovereign state and even minted his own currency. However, in the end, the lavish lifestyle he enjoyed did not afford him enough to pay his men, who soon began to desert him. The Spanish were aware of the deteriorating situation and organized an attack a month later to regain control of the island. MacGregor fled when he realized that he had lost the support of his men. Those remaining on the island were nevertheless successful in driving off the Spanish aggressors.

Just a few days after MacGregor's departure, a young privateer named Luis Aury came looking to join him. Aury was fortunate to have about 130 of his own soldiers and $60,000. Amelia was desperate for any sort of capital, and the people basically granted him military command of the island in exchange for some of his money. He raised the Mexican Rebel flag, a standard he had onboard his ship from a previous revolutionary undertaking. Under Aury, smuggling became even more prosperous in Fernandina. Unfortunately, his men fought openly and often with the island's other residents, making the United States nervous. Taking advantage of Aury's increasing problems, the United States forced him to surrender the island on December 23, 1817. The stars and stripes flew again.

Amelia grew into a more orderly society as part of the Florida Territory, which became a state in 1845. Soon after, Amelia's most influential resident, David Yulee, who was instrumental in Florida gaining statehood, made his mark. Yulee's plan was to build a railroad from Amelia Island to Cedar Key on the Gulf Coast. This would save ships the time and trouble of sailing around the Florida peninsula as their cargo could be shipped across the state much quicker by train and reloaded on a ship for distribution around the Gulf of Mexico. Yulee further envisioned a train across Mexico that would expedite shipping to the Pacific Ocean. Yulee completed his train across Florida but faced significant setbacks when the Civil War started a month after the train made its first run. When Florida seceded from the Union, Amelia Island flew the flag of the Confederacy, its eighth. Nevertheless, Fernandina made a comeback after the war, thanks in large part to Yulee's railroad.

Combined with the rich untapped resources of Florida's interior, the deep waters of Fernandina's harbor, and the railroad, Amelia Island became one of the leading ports in the South and the country. Many soldiers stationed around the island during the Civil War returned to capitalize on the potential they had seen and to enjoy the warmer weather. These people and others became very wealthy and made the island a leader in postwar economic recovery.

However, South Florida would develop into a more desirable tourist location as industry leaders soon discovered its offerings. Amelia's economy faded in the early part of the 20th century until the introduction of the paper mills and the shrimping industry stabilized it. The beautiful beaches slowly began to attract tourists again, and the town changed its name to Fernandina Beach in the 1950s, mostly as a marketing tool. In the 1970s, the Amelia Island Plantation was built, followed by the Ritz Carlton Amelia in 1991. Both of these organizations helped to further solidify the tourism industry, reestablish a strong economy, and add to the rich history of this small barrier island named Amelia.

One

PLACES

A fire destroyed much of Fernandina in 1876 and again in 1883. This picture is one of the very few photographs of Centre Street before those fires occurred. It was taken near the foot of the docks looking east. The building on the left was a grain and feed store that belonged to Maj. W. B. C. Duryee. He was instrumental in completing the Cumberland Island Jetty and saved the First Presbyterian Church bell from being converted into weapons during the Civil War. (Courtesy Florida State Archives.)

The home of David Yulee, once one of Amelia's most impressive homes, was located on the corner of Alachua and Third Streets. Yulee actually founded what is now downtown Fernandina Beach after deciding that Old Town, where most homes were located previously, was not an appropriate site to build his railroad terminal.

Samuel T. Riddell's home was located on North Fifth Street between Alachua and Broome Streets. Riddell was a member of the 7th New Hampshire Volunteers and settled in Fernandina after the Civil War. In 1879, he was appointed postmaster. Prior to that, he served as mayor of Fernandina during its worst yellow fever outbreak in 1877.

Villa Las Palmas stills stands as Fernandina's most celebrated home. The California mission–style mansion was built in 1910 for Nathanial B. Borden at 315 Alachua Street. Borden, a shipping and lumber agent, built the home as a wedding present for his 17-year-old bride, Flossie. Borden, incidentally, was 52, and the wedding was held in Cuba as Flossie's father did not approve of the marriage. Borden was one of early Fernandina's more vibrant personalities, and this grandiose home reflected that. After his death in 1938, the home was eventually sold to shrimper Harry Sahlman for $12,000.

The photograph at the top of this page is believed to show the original home of Samuel A. Swann, a local dignitary before the Civil War. It stood at the corner of Centre and Seventh Streets. His second home, pictured in the foreground of the lower picture, was nicknamed the Cottage Ornee and stood a block down from his original house at the corner of Centre and Sixth Streets. It was remodeled by Fernandina's most celebrated architect, Robert S. Schuyler, in 1882 and was perhaps the most impressive home on Centre Street. The woman standing on the porch in the upper photograph is most likely Swann's wife, Whitney.

Tennis Court at Residence of Sam D. Swann JB

"Buzzard Roost" Mr. Swann's yard

The Cottage Ornee was complete with tennis courts and an impressive tree house known as Buzzard Roost, a favorite of the Swann children and others in the neighborhood. Swann used the tennis courts to entertain other locals, as he was himself one of Fernandina's most important citizens. He originally came to Fernandina in 1855 as an accountant with the company contracted to build David Yulee's railroad. He eventually became the treasurer of the Florida Railroad Company and, after brokering the sale of mass tracts of Florida land, was probably the state's most knowledgeable real estate agent. Swann is one of the founders of St. Peter's Episcopal Church and was well liked throughout the town.

Behind the cat posed on the porch of this Amelia Island house is the home of Capt. Jones Davis, located at 421 North Third Street. Davis made a significant impact on the shrimping industry as the first captain ever to use a power-driven boat to drag his nets in deep water.

The second home of Major Duryee sat at the corner of Eighth and Centre Streets until it was razed in the 1950s to make room for a gas station. His first home still stands at the southwest corner of North Fifth and Broome Streets.

The Lesesne house still stands on Centre Street and is believed to be the oldest home on Amelia Island. The home was built in 1860 by John Lesesne. He would soon leave the island to treat injured soldiers during the Civil War. He never returned to Fernandina. The home was then purchased by John Friend in 1868. Friend went on to become the county judge and state senator.

Thomas Borden, the son of Nathanial Borden, stands on the porch of the offices of N. B. Borden and Company, located on Third Street. Thomas worked with his father's company. The women on the porch and children in the donkey cart are unidentified.

Another of the town's most spectacular homes was designed by Robert Schuyler and built for George Fairbanks in 1885. The home featured 20 elegant rooms, including a staircase made from Honduras mahogany and library bookcases made from wood grown in Fairbanks's own orange groves in Central Florida. In the 15-foot tower, Fairbanks's granddaughter sat in 1901 and watched the great fire of Jacksonville some 50 miles away. To keep warm, Fairbanks had 10 fireplaces with tiles featuring scenes from Shakespearian plays and *Aesop's Fables*. The house was home to Fernandina's first elevator, albeit more of a large dumbwaiter, and was among the very first homes on the island with a telephone and running water. The water used in the kitchen was rainwater collected in a cistern in the basement. The bathrooms drew water from a well provided by the city. It is currently a bed-and-breakfast inn.

O. S. Oakes established his business and this home c. 1883. He ran steam and lumber planing mills on Second Street and served as postmaster, city council president, and county undertaker. The latter was an appropriate role for him since his mills manufactured the majority of Fernandina's coffins. This home was located on North Fourth Street and was also home to Nathanial Borden while Villa Las Palmas was being built.

This home, located at 327 South Seventh Street, was originally built by the Hedges family, briefly owned by St. Peter's Episcopal Church, and eventually bought by W. Theo Waas in 1899. He remodeled the house considerably and doubled its living area. Waas, a well-known local physician, operated a drugstore at the corner of Centre and Fourth Streets.

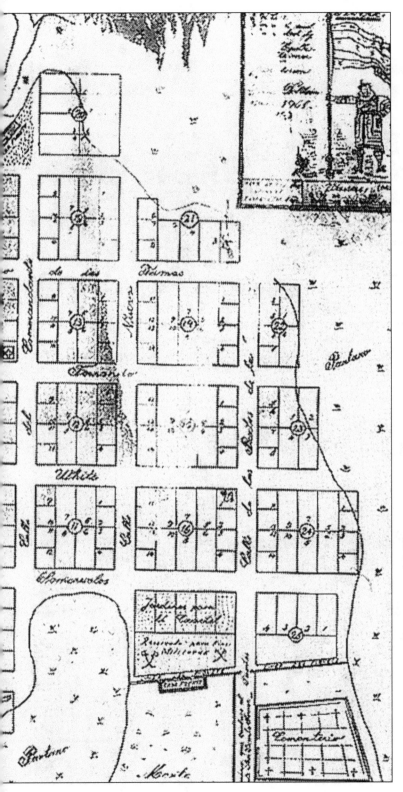

Prior to David Yulee's purchase of the Mattair-Fernandez estate and his master plan to create a "new" Fernandina, what is now known as Old Town served as the population center of Amelia Island. George Clarke, a Spanish loyalist and island resident, was charged by the Spanish governor to name and lay out the town. He used the 1573 Law of the Indies, which was used to create all new Spanish towns in the New World, to plat the town. Fernandina was the last town in the New World to be platted using this ancient code, a fact that is still taught in schools in Spain. This image shows the layout of Old Town with Fort San Carlos and the Amelia River to the west and the entrance to Egan's Creek to the north. (Courtesy Florida State Archives.)

After the town moved to its present location, Old Town grew into a mostly African American community. A boardwalk from Old Town to Fernandina was constructed across the marsh, and the land that is now home to the Smurfit-Stone Container paper mill. The boardwalk served as an important thoroughfare for African Americans traveling between home in Old Town and work in Fernandina. The above image shows the boardwalk looking north from Fernandina to Old Town and the lower picture is of the boardwalk looking south from Old Town to Fernandina.

This pilot tower was located in Old Town. Any ship that comes into port must have an experienced pilot onboard with knowledge of local waters. Before the advent of radio, harbor pilots used the tower to spot ships coming into port so they could meet them offshore.

This photograph was taken from the top of the pilot tower. It looks west towards the Amelia River. Many photographers in early Fernandina took advantage of the bird's-eye view the pilot tower offered.

The boardwalk from Old Town connected to Fernandina's North Second Street. This fact, and the street's proximity to the water, helped it rival Centre Street as Fernandina's busiest thoroughfare. The sign on the right advertising stoves belonged to W. P. Streety, whose business was ruined by fires. In fact, it was in Streety's shop that the fire of 1883 began.

At the northwest corner of Centre and Second Streets is a building originally built in 1878 for Josiah Prescott's shoe store. In 1903, the building was bought by Louis Hirth and opened as the Palace Saloon. Today the Palace Saloon is still in operation as the oldest continuously operating bar in Florida. It served as an ice cream parlor during Prohibition. Pictured here are Mr. Homage, right, a bartender, and Buck Lockwood, manager.

As did many saloons in the late 1800s and early 1900s, the Palace Saloon issued these tokens to customers. They were often given as change to assure patrons would return or were used to reward the most faithful of customers. The "H" on the left token in the bottom row stood for, of course, Hirth. (Courtesy Burgess Lewellen.)

Yulee hoped his railroad would bolster the tourist industry in Fernandina. His Florida Railroad Company built the Florida House as a hotel on South Third Street. It housed Union officers during the Civil War. Additions were built in 1865 and 1882 after the hotel was sold to Major Leddy, himself a former Union officer. It is the oldest continuously run hotel in Florida.

As the island grew as a tourist destination, the Florida Railroad Company decided a larger and more elegant hotel than the Florida House was needed. The Egmont Hotel opened its doors to the public on November 1, 1878. It stood at the corner of South Seventh and Beech Streets and was managed by B. H. and Samuel Skinner. It featured a bowling alley, billiard room, and tennis and croquet courts. It also offered heated rooms, hot and cold water baths on every floor, and telegraph and telephone connections. The hotel was torn down in 1901 when much of Florida's tourism moved farther south.

After the Egmont was torn down, a group of local businessmen, including Louis Hirth, realized the need for a hotel in the downtown area to keep the tourist industry alive. They constructed the 34-room Keystone Hotel in 1912 on the north side of Centre Street between Seventh and Eighth Streets. The hotel had extensive fountains and gardens behind it. The fountain that currently stands in front of the courthouse in Fernandina is a replica of one of those. The hotel was torn down in 1972, spurring another public response, this time to protect Fernandina's historic architecture.

The Albemarle House was a hotel that primarily served boat captains who came into port. It sat between North Fourth and Fifth Streets on Broome Street and at one point was among Fernandina's tallest buildings.

This photograph was taken sometime around 1891 from atop the Egmont Hotel and looks northeast. The steeple under construction belongs to the Trinity United Methodist Church, whose congregation dates back to 1822 and who originally gathered in the homes of church members. This building was constructed at the corner of South Eighth and Ash Streets. In the center of the photograph stands the city water tower.

Fernandina's waterworks helped to modernize the town. Built in response to the fires that had previously destroyed many local buildings, the facilities featured a water tank that was 50 feet wide in diameter and 100 feet high. The water, propelled by natural pressure from an artesian well 650 feet deep, discharged 1,500 gallons of water per minute. The city also established the Fernandina Brush and Light Company, which provided electric lights to streets and businesses.

This photograph provides a view of downtown Fernandina looking west from the water tower. St. Peter's Episcopal Church sits to the left. Its congregation originally met in the building in the center of this photograph's foreground. When the church's present structure was built at the northeast corner of Eighth and Centre Streets in 1881, this entire building was moved a bit north and given to its African American parishioners. (Courtesy Florida State Archives.)

rst Presbyterian Church and 6th Street.
FERNANDINA, Fla.

The First Presbyterian Church, built in 1860 on land donated by David Yulee, remains the oldest church on the island and is among the oldest in the state. During the Civil War, its sanctuary was used as a primary school. (Courtesy Florida State Archives.)

From Centre Street looking down South Fifth Street, from front to back, the Allan, Fishler, and Suhrer houses are visible. Fernando L. Suhrer, the victim of one of Fernandina's earliest and most notorious murders, was shot by the great-great-grandson of Thomas Jefferson, Thomas Jefferson Epps, on the steps of the inn Suhrer managed. Epps erroneously accused Suhrer of making a disparaging remark about his wife.

This photograph peers along North Sixth Street at what was known as the Silk Stocking District. The homes pictured here belonged to, from front to back, the Hirths, Lukenbilles, and Chadwicks. Louis Hirth was the proprietor of the Palace Saloon. The Lukenbille house burned and was replaced by a home for Dr. D. G. Humphreys. Steven Chadwick owned several tugboats used to assist ships coming into the harbor.

A cart used to extinguish fires sits in the shadows on the right side of this photograph of South Seventh Street, taken from Centre Street. The trolley tracks made their way down South Seventh Street to the home of Effingham Bailey, who was part owner of the trolley.

Looking down Ash Street from South Sixth Street, the home of William Jeffreys, who moved to the island in 1864, can be seen. Jeffreys helped found the Bank of Fernandina, which would become the First National Bank of Fernandina. He also helped build the Chandlery Building (also known as the Hoyt Building) across North Second Street from the Palace Saloon.

The Memorial United Methodist Church was built on Centre Street in 1930. This building, however, was at least the third for the congregation whose history on the island dates back to the early 1820s.

Small dogs like this one were a common feature on early Fernandina streets. This image was taken at the Catholic property beginning at North Fourth and Broome Streets. The property was home to St. Michael's Roman Catholic Church and the Convent of the Sisters of St. Joseph.

St. Michael's Roman Catholic Church, built in 1872, replaced a wood structure that stood in the same location. Catholicism was no stranger to Amelia Island as the Spanish had introduced Catholic missions to the Native Americans 300 years earlier. (Courtesy Florida State Archives.)

The small chapel inside St. Joseph's Academy had ornately painted ceilings and an impressive alter for a chapel its size.

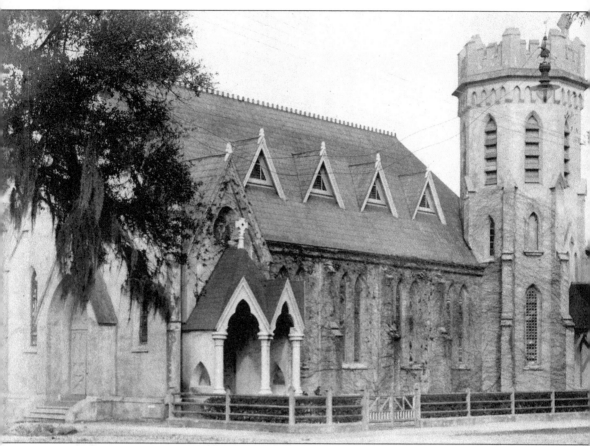

St. Peter's Episcopal Church, located at the northeast corner of Centre and Eighth Street, is perhaps
the most impressive piece of architecture on Centre Street. The church was originally formed
by the Reverend Owen P. Thackera in 1858. Church fathers soon bought a small parcel of land
from the Florida Railroad for $200 and built the small church pictured on page 27. Thackera left
Fernandina during the Civil War and, upon his return, found the church in disrepair. With some
of Fernandina's most notable citizens, such as Swann, Duryee, and Fairbanks, as parishioners, he
was eventually able to convince Robert Schuyler to design a new structure, and the cornerstone
for this building was laid on August 10, 1881. It was finished in 1884.

Schuyler's original design for the church featured an interesting tower. The original tower would eventually be destroyed by fire. However, most of the rest of the building remains just as Schuyler depicted it in this conceptual sketch. (Courtesy Florida State Archives.)

Two unidentified women sit on the steps outside St. Peter's Episcopal Church. The church's first service in this building was hastily held on March 30, 1884, to suit Mrs. H. D. Huntington, a wealthy traveler from Cincinnati staying at the Egmont Hotel. In return for the church holding services before it was fully completed, she donated the chancel windows.

This photograph of St. Peter's interior was taken sometime after 1893 when the Harrison pipe organ was installed at a cost of $2,000. Its casing is made of curly pine, which is actually a rare pattern in the pine caused by a deformity. Several of the alter pieces feature this beautiful hardwood. The pews were designed by Schuyler and originally cost $6.50 apiece. Most of the windows were made by Edward Colegate of New York City at a cost of approximately $175 apiece. After the original windows were damaged by fire, Colegate reproduced them with a few changes suggested by Samuel Swann. Swann even convinced him to reduce his cost from the originals. Many of the windows are memorials to some of Fernandina's most beloved citizens. The roof has a unique design of open timber and was patterned after the inverted hull of a ship to reflect Fernandina's seafaring spirit.

Stacks of lumber are seen in the distance in this photograph of Alachua Street taken at North Fifth Street. The building on the left is the First Baptist Church. This building was completed in 1888 after the original was burned the previous year. A larger brick building later replaced this wood frame church.

This is the brick building that replaced the older and smaller First Baptist Church. It was built in 1925 and was a necessity as the congregation outgrew the other building. The church's continued expansion has taken them to South Eighth Street.

Looking east from atop the Egmont Hotel, one can see the Macedonia African Methodist Episcopal Church to the right. It was founded in 1870 by Samuel Irving of Philadelphia. The tracks that run down Beech Street in this photograph carried guests of the Egmont Hotel to the Strathmore Hotel and the beach. The house in the center foreground is the Bell House. Built by Capt. James Bell in 1889, the building is sometimes referred to as the C House and is home to the Beech Street Grill today. James and his twin brother, William, built no fewer than nine homes in Fernandina. The best known was built in Old Town at 212 Estrada Street by William in 1888. It commands an impressive view of the Amelia River and the Plaza de San Carlos. It is known as the Captains House and most recently the Pippi House after it was used as the home of the title character in the 1988 motion picture *The Adventures of Pippi Longstocking*. The long building in this photograph held a bowling alley.

The New Zion Missionary Baptist Church, also founded in 1870, stands in the foreground as another one of Fernandina's earliest black churches. The building in this picture burned down in 1904 and was rebuilt at the same site on the corner of Atlantic Avenue and South Tenth Street. The steeple in the background belongs to another early black church, the First Missionary Baptist Church. Located on South Ninth Street, it was founded in 1860. The steeple pictured here was removed in 1958. Beyond the church is the Egmont Hotel. Beside the New Zion Missionary Baptist Church on Atlantic Avenue is Public School No. 1. The school represents another example of Robert Schuyler's design and was built in 1886. The school consisted of four classrooms and was used until 1927.

This new Public School No. 1 replaced the old one when it opened on January 1, 1928, across the street and slightly east on Atlantic Avenue. The school served white children in Fernandina until a new high school was built in 1955. The building now serves as the district offices of the Nassau County School Board.

Fernandina's black children received their education at Peck High School from 1927 until 1969, when desegregation occurred. This building is now a community center. Rufus Johnson stands on the steps of Peck High School here in the 1930s. (Courtesy Florida State Archives.)

Taken around 1900, this photograph of Centre Street, at the intersection of Fourth Street, shows the epicenter of early Fernandina. Centre Street remains an important business center in Fernandina and Nassau County today. Note the horse and buggy approaching the city docks in the distance and the power cables above the street.

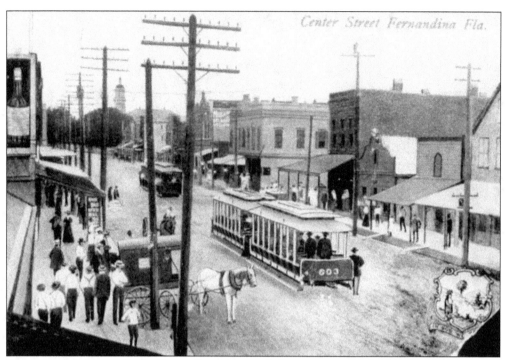

This postcard shows a lively Centre Street scene. It depicts a typical day in Fernandina during its Golden Age as tourists and locals flocked downtown and business boomed. (Courtesy Florida State Archives.)

The Swann building stands at the northwest corner of Centre and Fourth Streets and is adorned with a pressed-metal exterior. Samuel Swann further exemplified his dedication to the town of Fernandina as he constructed this building with space for the town's first public library, a ballroom, and gymnasium. This structure, built in 1890, also housed Waas's drugstore on the first floor. The city fire bell was located behind the building.

This establishment was built by Fred Hoyt, who moved to Fernandina from New Hampshire in 1879. It served as a grocery and ship chandlery and is still located at the northeast corner of Centre and Second Streets. D. A. and William Kelly eventually took possession of the building and turned it into one of Fernandina's premier retail stores. A third story was added to the original in 1901.

Hoyt went on to partner with William Jeffreys to form the highly successful First National Bank in 1887. The Hoyt house, pictured here, was built across from St. Peter's Episcopal Church at the southeast corner of Centre and South Eighth Streets. It was modeled after the Rockefellers' cottage on Jekyll Island.

This building at the corner of South Sixth and Ash Streets belonged to William Lohman. The German immigrant originally erected the building to house a dry goods store in 1890 but later sold furniture there. He served as a county commissioner and married the daughter of Major Suhrer, the innkeeper who was killed by Thomas Jefferson Epps. (Courtesy Florida State Archives.)

The Hardee building, home of the Fernandina Development Company in this photograph, sits at the southwest corner of Centre and Third Streets. It now houses Fernandina's Fantastic Fudge. Originally known as City Mart, it was later a hardware store operated by Noble, Ira, and John Hardee. Noble Anthony Hardee married a young woman from Murfreesboro, Tennessee, named Emma Love. She went on to become one of Fernandina's first female community leaders through her work with the First Presbyterian Church and the town's needy children. One of the town's elementary schools now bears her name.

Daniel and John Mularkey, twin brothers pictured here, bought this dry goods business from the Mode brothers in 1897. This transaction was very convenient as "MB" was already engraved on the building's columns. The boxes to the right likely held food brought from New York via steamship. Although this building still stands at 210 Centre Street, the second story has been removed.

This photograph was taken c. 1914 and features Fernandina's trolley. Many of Fernandina's citizens and tourists used the trolley to get from downtown to the beach via Centre and Beech Streets. The train in the background is adorned with banners advertising a picnic.

As Centre Street crosses Eighth Street, it becomes Atlantic Avenue and leads to the Atlantic Ocean. This photograph was taken from atop the city's water tower and looks towards the beach. To the right is Central Park. The home in the center, currently Oxley Heard Funeral Home, was built in 1891 and belonged to Dr. John Denham Palmer. He was a surgeon in the Civil War and played an important role during the town's yellow fever outbreak of 1877. The public school that opened in 1928 used the large field shown in the foreground as its lawn. The Amelia Island Lighthouse is visible in the distance.

A saltwater marsh known as Egan's Creek cuts through the center of the island. The Amelia Island Lighthouse is located on the west side of the creek. At close to one-quarter mile from the coast, it is the inland-most lighthouse on the Eastern Seaboard. The other structure in the photograph was the home of the lighthouse keeper.

By the 1920s when this photograph was taken, Atlantic Avenue had been paved all the way to the beach and cut across Egan's Creek, seen at left. Egan's Creek was named after Stephen Egan, the caretaker of an English indigo plantation located on the island in the 1700s. In the 1940s, the Army Corp of Engineers installed gates that prevented the flow of saltwater south of Atlantic Avenue. New gates were installed in 2004 that allowed saltwater to flow through them, and part of the island was able to reclaim its original state. (Courtesy P. K. Yonge Library of Florida History.)

Many of Fernandina's citizens spent their weekends in recreation at the beach. The easiest way to get there was by taking the trolley. This photograph depicts a group of beachgoers as they arrive at the Atlantic Ocean, perhaps a little overdressed by today's standards.

In the late 19th century, the primary structure at the beach was the Strathmore Hotel, built in 1882 by the Florida Railroad Company. It represents another of Robert Schuyler's designs and was located where Beech Street met the Atlantic Ocean. The Strathmore and its sister, the Egmont, were instrumental in developing the tourist industry in Fernandina—especially as an ocean retreat.

The majority of the Strathmore Hotel was destroyed by a hurricane in 1898. In its place, a pavilion and casinos were constructed that were served by the trolley from downtown. These businesses were very popular and regularly brought tourists and locals alike to the beach. The casino featured a bowling alley (the island's second) and porches that offered scenic views of the ocean. Both establishments were also known for their food and were among the town's most popular eateries. The picture above was taken c. 1920 and features the trolley in the left background and several cars on what must of have been a busy day for the casino.

Many people who came to the beach did so for the sun, sand, and surf rather than the casinos. As a result, a bathhouse, pictured here in the foreground, was constructed that allowed beachgoers the opportunity to change or rinse off in private. The casino is visible in the background.

By the 1920s, a small radio station, the island's first, was constructed on the beach. This radio station broadcast its signal to the north end of the island. The city included it in promotional materials as an indication that Fernandina kept pace with modern trends. (Courtesy P. K. Yonge Library of Florida History.)

The tourist industry eventually rebounded and continued to develop on the island. The Seaside Inn, built in the mid-1940s, included a popular restaurant. This building spent many years as the most popular hotel on Amelia Island's beaches. (Courtesy Florida State Archives.)

When home construction first began on the beaches, houses were built by those who took a chance on land they did not own. The government owned most of the dunes, and the beach was not valued as the prime real estate it is today. As things changed and tastes evolved, the beach became privatized, and many homes like these were constructed in the 1920s.

Until the early part of the 1900s, the southern end of Amelia Island had few residents save the area around the western side of the island and the entrance to Harrison Creek known as Harrison Plantation. The plantation, seen here, employed many slaves, who grew Sea Island cotton. When Union troops landed here in 1862, they released the slaves, who settled the nearby area known as Franklin Town.

American Beach was established in 1935 after the Afro-American Life Insurance Company enjoyed many beach retreats at Franklin Town. It would eventually grow into a prominent African American beach community. Many of the descendants of the original landowners still live here. The beach is also home to some of Amelia's only unmolested dunes, pictured here. These are part of the Timucuan Ecological and Historic Preserve.

In the 1940s, Gustave Gerbing created Gerbing Gardens on the banks of the Amelia River near Amelia City. The grounds were planted with an array of flora and visited by tourists and locals. This photograph depicts an aerial view of the gardens.

Just down Gerbing Road from the gardens, also on the banks of the Amelia River, was this popular swimming area. Many of the locals, looking to avoid the wave action of the beach or oyster beds in other parts of the river, chose this location as their favorite swimming hole.

Construction of Fort Clinch on the northernmost point of Amelia Island began in 1842. However, after the invention of the rifled cannon, the fort became obsolete before it was even finished. In fact, it remained unfinished when Union forces occupied it 1862 after the Confederacy surrendered it without firing a shot. The fort saw no action during the war, and Union forces worked to finish its construction to pass the time. As seen here, sand had overtaken much of the fort by the 1930s until the Civilian Conservation Corps restored it. In 1935, Fort Clinch became one of Florida's first state parks.

As the town of Fernandina grew, so did the neighborhoods between downtown and the beach. This picture looks along South Fifteenth Street from Beech Street and was taken sometime in the early 1950s.

This photograph was taken in April 1949 and looks down North Eighteenth Street from Highland Street. The island's steepest hill, known locally as the Eighteenth Street hill, rises in the background. Construction on houses here began shortly after this photograph was taken, and the road now serves as one of the main entrances into one of Fernandina's most established neighborhoods.

While it is best known for its tourism, Amelia is no stranger to other industries. This mill, built at the mouth of Egan's Creek in 1865, was known as Reed's Mill. It processed much of the lumber that came through Fernandina.

The phosphate elevator at the foot of Franklin Street was used to process the phosphate mined from Florida's interior in the late 1800s and early 1900s. Phosphate is heavy and thus requires a deep port for shipping. Fernandina was the only U.S. port that shipped phosphate until the Tampa Bay port was dredged in the 1930s.

Two

PEOPLE

The first people to settle Amelia Island were the Timucuan Indians around 2000 BC. They called the island Napoyca and grew corn, beans, pumpkins, and squash. They also fished and gathered shellfish. The tall Native Americans with high hairstyles must have been an intimidating sight for the much shorter Europeans who first landed here in 1562. (Courtesy Florida State Archives.)

When the British took possession of Florida in the 1700s, they gave away most of it to British citizens in the form of land grants. The Second Earl of Egmont, John Percival, was given Amelia Island. Percival never actually came to the island but did operate an indigo plantation here. He called the island Egmont and established a small settlement at the site of Old Town called Egmont Town.

After changing possession between the French, Spanish, and English over the course of two and a half centuries, Amelia would soon change hands several more times in a matter of a few short years. In late June 1817, Gregor MacGregor seized the island under the auspices of liberating Florida from Spanish control. He flew a flag with a green cross over the island. However, MacGregor was short on money, and when he was unable to pay his troops, they deserted him. With no force to sustain his rule on the island, he soon left. (Courtesy Florida State Archives.)

After MacGregor departed, Luis Aury, a young Frenchman previously involved in efforts to liberate Mexico from Spanish control, came to Amelia in mid-September. Aury paid off MacGregor's men and raised the flag of the Mexican revolutionaries over the island. He declared himself ruler of the island and promoted Amelia Island as a launching point for smugglers into the United States. Aury attempted to establish a legitimate government on the island and even held elections. He planned to write a constitution. However, before that could be accomplished, Pres. James Monroe and Congress acted to reoccupy the island, and on December 23, 1817, Aury surrendered Amelia to U.S. forces. (Courtesy Florida State Archives.)

Those for whom Fernandina and the island it sits on were named never visited the island. Fernandina was named after the Spanish Catholic monarch Ferdinand VII of Spain, who reigned from 1814 to 1833. The name was suggested by east Florida governor Enrique White after Fernandina resident George Clarke platted the township.

The island was given its name by James Oglethorpe, founder of Savannah and English governor of the colony of Georgia in the early 1700s. After a visit to the island, he named it after Princess Amelia Sophia Elenora, daughter of King George II of England. Known for her beauty, she nevertheless lived a quiet life and died childless in 1786 as the last living child of her parents.

David Yulee is pictured here as a young man and later as an older gentleman. He, perhaps, had more impact on Amelia Island than any other person. He was born David Levy to a Sephardic Jewish family of Moroccan descent. He was well educated and studied law under future Florida governor Raymond Reid. Yulee was instrumental in the effort to establish Florida's statehood and helped pen the state constitution. He went on to become Florida's first senator and the first Jewish senator in the United States. He changed his name, however, from Levy to Yulee to avoid anti-Semitism. The brains behind the Florida Railroad Company, Yulee convinced the citizens of Fernandina to move from Old Town to present-day Fernandina, which better suited this endeavor. He personally purchased the Mattair-Fernandez estate in order for this to happen and platted the new town there. Yulee's first train ran on March 1, 1861, but was short-lived as the Civil War began a month later. (Courtesy Florida State Archives.)

Joseph Finnegan also played an important role in Fernandina's history. He came to the island with Yulee as the contractor to build the railroad. He was to be paid from the sale of land owned by the railroad after its completion. However, after the outbreak of war virtually destroyed real estate in the South, Finnegan found himself bankrupt. In retaliation, he publicized letters he received from Senator Yulee that extolled the virtues of secession by the state prior to the Civil War. This led to Yulee's incarceration for treason. Before his bankruptcy, Finnegan built a 40-room mansion on the island between North Eleventh and Twelfth Streets. During the war, he served in the Confederate army and eventually rose to the rank of general. When he returned to Fernandina afterward, he found that his home had been taken over by the Freedman's Bureau. It no longer stands. (Courtesy Florida State Archives.)

Like Finnegan, many of the men who shaped Fernandina's history during its golden age served during the Civil War. This picture was taken at a reunion of some local veterans. The only identifiable person, George Latham, stands fourth from left. He was one of the port's original harbor pilots. His son, J. W., became harbormaster and had an office on Second Street.

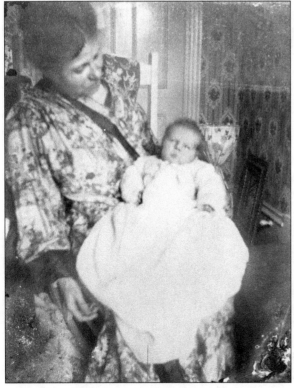

Many of those who first came to Fernandina as soldiers during the war returned to start their families. As a result, a healthy economy began to develop and the population quickly rose. This photograph depicts Lucy Golding Starbucks Davis holding young William Jones Davis Jr., who later died at the age of 19 months.

Susie Jones Davis, sister of William Jones Davis Jr., holds a box of chewing gum given to her for her birthday.

Pictured here is one of the Kelly children. This might have been taken at the Kelly family home, located at 214 South Seventh Street. The home was originally built by Samuel Swann for his son. Note the mosquito net around the bed in the background. This would have been necessary before air-conditioning was available when windows were left open for circulation. Without the nets, the mosquitoes would have had a feast.

The children of Daniel Mularkey, who owned the dry goods store, enjoyed dressing up in costumes and having play dates just as children do today. Pictured here from left to right are Dan Mularkey, Wheeler Mularkey, King Mularkey, and Mary Mularkey.

Cowboys and Indians must have been a popular game for children of the 19th century in Fernandina. Flip Roux, son of postmaster Elmer Roux, poses here as a cowboy. Flip's extensive costume collection must have been the envy of many of the other local children as several photographs exist of him in other costumes, including a Native American and a fireman.

These unidentified boys from Fernandina do not appear to be in costume. However, for children of the early 20th century on the island, their dress and unusual hairstyles were no doubt peculiar.

When the children were not attending parties, they had other toys to play with. This child was a member of the Borden family and is pictured here holding a Steiff teddy bear. Today original Steiff bears in good condition have been appraised at as much as $86,000.

The appropriately named Horsey sisters, Francis and Anita, take out a pony cart for play on North Fourth Street in 1900. Their father was the proprietor of Horsey and Company Druggist and Physician, located on the north side of Centre Street, near Second Street.

Well-dressed brother and sister Charles and Louise Lasserre pose at Gerbing's Oyster Bar. The oyster bar was another part of Gerbing's recreational grounds along the banks of the Amelia River toward the south end of the island.

Many of Fernandina's blacks worked in the households of the wealthier white families. Their children often played with the children of their employers. This young girl is pictured on the porch of the Johnson residence with a doll.

Many African American families lived in Old Town after most of the white residents moved to the new Fernandina. Note the outhouse and small puppy visible in the background.

These two pictures represent nearly all of the white school-aged population of Fernandina around the turn of the 20th century. These photographs show the student bodies of the public school and the primary private school on the island. The above picture was taken in 1898 at Public School No. 1 on Atlantic Avenue. A total of 48 students and teachers appear in the picture. Below, the class of Sister Agnes at St. Joseph's Academy poses for a photograph taken around the same time. There are 63 students and teachers here.

The graduating classes at Public School No. 1 were small. This is the senior class of 1924. From left to right are (first row) Susie Davis, Lucille Peace, Mary Hughes, and Lucy Nolan; (second row) Evelyn Galphin, Lola Bunker, and Kate Waas; (third row) Will Sims, Mary Frances Silva, and Dorothy Strickland.

After the new Public School No. 1 opened, the island's public school students moved across the street. Pictured here is the freshman class of 1929, among the first students to attend the new school. From left to right are (first row) two unidentified, N. A. Hardee, Gail Longee, I. D. Hardee, and George Johnson; (second row) Charles Higginbotham, Jake Bunch, and Hale Sheffield; (third row) Elizabeth Van Brunt, Ruth Humphreys, Elizabeth Boring, Mildred Beugnet, Margaret Haverstick, Roselle Jones, and unidentified; (fourth row) ? Skipper, Lois Lowe, Alice Saunders, and three unidentified.

Athletics played a major role in local activities. By the late 1800s, baseball had quickly grown into one of America's favorite sports. Many smaller teams began to form around the country, often put together by businesses that competed against other teams from a given industry. Fernandina was not immune to the sport's growing popularity, and the Fernandina Baseball Club was likely formed with the help of local businesses. This is especially true of the above picture, which is probably the earlier of the two and features what appears to be more of a rag-tag group of players. A small boy stands in as their mascot. The team in the bottom photograph was crowned champions of Florida in 1894. The team posed in front of an interesting mural and displayed some early baseball equipment. They are Frank Maxwell, Jimme Nix, Henry Hobein, Wallace Maxwell, Jonnie Sauls, Chas Hernandez, Edwin Williams, John McGiffin, Frank Williams, Gus Macdonell, and Fritz Hobein.

Football also enjoyed popularity in Fernandina. As in baseball, the town had their own club team, seen here in 1908. Pictured are, from left to right, (first row) Fred Hill, Ralph Wolff, Wilber Mahoney, W. Raymond Wolff, "Dutch" Emile Rutishauer, and Pat Murphy; (second row) Raymond McDonald, Bill Seibert, J. D. Palmer (coach), John Partridge, Lewis Thompson, Gene McDonald, Cliff Hiller, Tiny Wiemer, Luther Mursharm, and Harold Mann (coach and captain).

This is the first basketball team ever to take the floor for a Fernandina high school. The team members were, from left to right, (first row) A. Jones and Jackson Mizell; (second row) Louis A. Ferreira, Clayton Hughes, and Louis Nolan; (third row) John Kline, Joseph Dana, Flip Roux, William Fishler, and William Sims. The photograph was taken in 1925.

Beyond baseball, football, and basketball, there were plenty of other recreational activities on the island. The men pictured here enjoyed skeet shooting from a platform on the beach built for that purpose. Note the many shotgun shells scattered on the dock.

Sometimes the people on Amelia preferred to shoot more than just skeet. As much of the island was wooded, opportunities for hunting were ample. Here two unidentified local men return from a hunting trip with a deer they killed on the island. Others hunted for birds or small game like armadillo or raccoon.

With fertile waters surrounding them, many island residents enjoyed fishing. These two unidentified men caught 27 drum in one day before posing for this picture on the docks at the Fernandina harbor.

Gus Gerbing pulled this shark out of the Amelia River—apparently without much tackle. He caught it near his family's property close to what is now known as Amelia City on the island's south end.

This young man caught a rather impressive shark in the waters around Fernandina and hoisted it on the city docks to weigh it. The shark measured 9 feet and weighed 820 pounds. With fish like shark, grouper, red fish, drum, sheepshead, whiting, and barracuda, as well as other marine life like crabs, shrimp, turtles, dolphins, and manatees, creatures of the sea have always been an important part of life on Amelia Island. Industries associated with local sea life also served a key role in its economy. As seen by the size of this shark, the life Amelia's waters have produced are on no small scale. In 1961, the world-record goliath grouper, previously known as the jewfish, was caught right off the city docks. It weighed 680 pounds.

Some of the meat produced in Fernandina was sold at the meat counter inside Island City Market. It was located in the store at the southwest corner of Centre and Third Streets and eventually became the Hardee brothers' hardware store and later Fantastic Fudge. The meat in this photograph includes poultry, pork, and sausage.

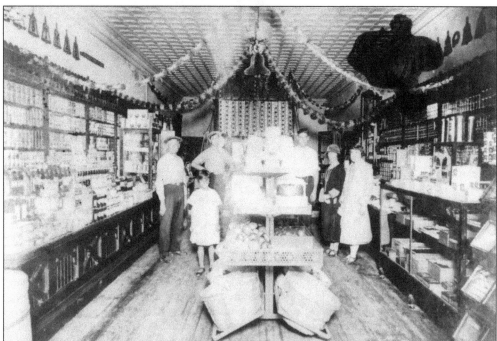

Another view inside Island City Market features some of the goods sold in the store as well as, from left to right, proprietor Fritz Hobein, Myrtle Moore, Carl Burges, Tommy Franks, and two unidentified women.

Other leisure activities around the island included the arts, and music was no exception. The 12-member metropolitan band of Fernandina poses here in front of a sand dune at the beach. The band would have played at parades and other exciting events happening in town.

When this picture was taken in 1894, the group called themselves the Fernandina Quartette Club despite the fact they numbered more than four. They were, from left to right, (first row) Alex McDaniel, Frank Williams, and ? MacDonnell; (second row) unidentified, Felix Livingston, Bill Roux, and Frank Latham. They pose in front of the same backdrop used by the championship baseball team.

St. Peter's Episcopal Church Choir, Fernandina, Florida. 19[0]

Some of the same musically gifted young men in the Fernandina Quartette Club also sang in the St. Peter's Episcopal Church Choir. This picture, taken on Easter Sunday 1900, included, from left to right, (first row) Tom ?, ? White, Roy Kennard, Jim Silva, Ed Thompson, Hawks Thompson, Archie Williams, and Jamie McNair; (second row) Wilson Boltzell, Mrs. Hillyer, Sophia Carrio, Louise Edson, Johanna Heckel, Francis Carrio, and Annie Baer; (third row) ? Williams, Florrie Livingston, Kate Williams, Major Duryee, Fritz Hobein, Jim Williams, Bishop E. G. Weed, unidentified, ? Preston, ? Grunwald, Judge Charles Hillyer, Tom Clarke, ? Silva, Hedges Thompson, and Belle Preston; (fourth row) Frank Williams, Felix Livingston, Bill Roux, ? Warfield, ? Hillyer, and unidentified; (with cross) Ed Hopkins. Judge Hillyer originally came to Fernandina as a customs agent. In addition to sitting as county judge, he served as tax collector and city councilman and was responsible for building a number of the houses of Fernandina.

76

Horses were an important aspect of early island life as they were the primary means of transportation. This horse and cart carries Liz and Anthony Brady in downtown Fernandina. The umbrella advertises P. R. Brady furniture and the opportunity to buy with credit.

As seen here, horse and buggies often took Fernandina residents down to the beach. The surrey with the fringe on top carries Lisa Brady. Elmer Roux poses on the left. The other two gentlemen are unidentified.

LIVERY, SALE & BOARDING STABLE,

BROOME STREET, FERNANDINA, Fla.
G. F. AVERY, PROPRIETOR.

Many of the town's hardworking horses may have been kept at G. F. Avery's Livery, located on Broome Street. This poster from sometime in the 1880s advertises that business. (Courtesy Florida State Archives.)

The fort at the northern tip of the island was named after Duncan Lamont Clinch, a commander during the First and Second Seminole Wars. Clinch did not spend much time on Amelia, if he ever even set foot on the island at all. Most of his work was accomplished in South Georgia and around the Apalachicola River to the west.

The fort that still bears General Clinch's name was a popular place to have picnics. Such was the case with the young group seen here sitting on portions of the fort. They are, from left to right, Arthur Steil, Florence Wolff, Maurice Kelly, Elise Steil, unidentified, Irene Steil, Theo Kelly, and unidentified. The Steil family owned the Atlantic Pavilion at Main Beach.

Some people did not bring their picnic to the beach; they found it when they got there. This group enjoys clamming and crabbing on the beach of Amelia Island. Rakes were used to turn up the sand and produce clams. The woman on the left holds a string that is baited to attract crabs. After she found a crab feeding on her bait, she would have used a net to scoop it up.

With seven other associates, Abraham Lincoln Lewis founded what would become the Afro-American Life Insurance in 1901. He eventually became president of the company, which thrived under his guidance. As a result, he became the first black millionaire in the state of Florida. Lewis's wife, Mary, was a native of Fernandina, and the popularity of his company's outings to Franklin Town convinced him to establish American Beach—the African American beach community on Amelia. The area comprised 200 acres that Lewis platted to include homes and businesses, which consisted of restaurants, hotels, and nightclubs. He named the streets for founders of the company and his family members. On sunny summer weekends in the mid-1900s, the beach was among the most crowded in Florida as one of the few that allowed African Americans. Lewis went on to found the Negro Business League in Jacksonville and contributed heavily to local black colleges. (Courtesy Florida State Archives.)

Back in town, Arthur Simmons, better known as the Ox Man, operated as something like a mobile flea market. He gathered items that people discarded and carried them around town with this ox and cart and sold them to people who were in need of the items.

The city of Fernandina had its own official municipal services that were responsible for trash collection. In July 1949, the town took delivery of this brand-new Ford V8 trash truck. The truck's crew poses with it. They are, from left to right, B. F. Snipe, Noah Vanzant, T. J. Crosby (driver), and John Howard.

Samuel Swann was one of the few men capable of rivaling David Yulee's impact on Fernandina. He moved to Fernandina at the age of 23 from Wilmington, North Carolina, to work as an accountant for Joseph Finnegan and the Florida Railroad Company. Eventually he was promoted and took charge of the company's landholdings. This job made him among the most prominent real estate agents in the state's history, as he was responsible for the sale of millions of Florida acres. Swann was so knowledgeable about Florida real estate that the state ultimately hired him to sell public land. He quickly became one of the town's most prominent and wealthy citizens. He used his wealth for the good of Fernandina and was well known for his philanthropy. As a result, the city named a fire engine after him in 1884. He died in 1909 and is buried in St. Peter's cemetery.

Those who used the Samuel A. Swann chemical fire engine would have been one of the island's volunteer firefighting groups like Tiger Company One, seen here. This picture was taken in 1892 where the group was stationed on North Third Street. Notice the group has weaved their name into the palm fronds in the back.

One of Fernandina's volunteer fire departments practices pulling a cart carrying hose through the city. There are nine people pulling the cart and two pushing it.

With the prominence of area churches, religious leaders were important figures on the island. Fr. Patrick Halligan, rector at St. Michael's Catholic Church from 1933 to 1952, poses here with his dogs.

Many of the descendants of the O'Hagan clan, pictured here, still live on the island today. They were best known as the keepers of the Amelia Island Lighthouse and lived in the small structure in the photograph. The lighthouse was originally constructed on Cumberland Island, Georgia, and moved brick by brick to Amelia in 1838.

George Fairbanks moved to Florida in 1842 and was quickly elected as a state senator. Working with the federal government, he was responsible for the land purchase that would become Fort Clinch. Fairbanks served in the Confederate army as a major in the Army of Tennessee. After that, David Yulee asked him to come to Fernandina to serve in the position he was perhaps best known for, editor of the local paper, the *Florida Mirror*. He was an avid historian and wrote what many consider to be the definitive book on early Florida history, *History of Florida*. He learned Spanish in order to properly research old archives for this project. Fairbanks went on to found the Florida Historical Society and served as its president. He also founded the University of the South in Sewanee, Tennessee, and served as president of the Florida Fruit Growers Association. His large 20-room home at the corner of South Seventh and Date Streets was known as Fairbanks' Folly.

Although he never lived there, Henry Flagler has his place in Fernandina history, albeit a dubious one. In the late 1800s, Flagler constructed a railroad that took tourists deeper into South Florida than had previously been possible. He developed many resorts along the way, including the grandiose Hotel Ponce de Leon in St. Augustine. Unfortunately, Flagler's rails bypassed Fernandina, which had previously served as the gateway to the state. This moved tourists to other parts of the state and helped spell the end of Amelia Island's golden age.

Three

EVENTS

Before its end, the golden age of Amelia Island was a period of incredible growth and commerce. The Nassau County courthouse was built in 1892 and has been the signature of Fernandina's historic downtown ever since. It is one of the oldest and finest examples of Victorian courthouses in the state, if not the country. It has been home to many significant events on Amelia, including a stirring campaign speech by William Jennings Bryan.

A replica of a fountain that was located in the gardens behind the Keystone Hotel currently resides in front of the courthouse. This photograph shows the original fountain and some of the guests who enjoyed it.

The train depot represented another very important building in Fernandina. This building, the third depot built on this site, still stands as a significant aspect of the downtown landscape. Constructed in 1899, it served passengers until the 1930s. The building currently houses a tourist information center for the chamber of commerce. (Courtesy Florida State Archives.)

City hall, located at the corner of South Second and Ash Streets, was originally built shortly after Yulee's railroad came to Fernandina. It included an impressive bell tower. In addition to city offices, it housed a fire station, police station, and jail. The building still stands, but several significant changes have been made. As fire engines became larger and more office space was needed, the single story that housed the engines in this photograph was eventually remodeled to include a second story. The bell tower was also removed. It remains the hub of city business, but fire and police operations have moved elsewhere.

As the town grew, a new post office was needed. In 1907, land was purchased on Centre Street, and ground was broken in 1909 for the new post office and customhouse across the street from the courthouse. The above photograph was taken looking north on December 16, 1909. The photograph below was taken on June 9, 1910, as the building was nearing completion. The post office, the first steel structure in town, held a federal courtroom where smugglers were tried during Prohibition.

With the growth in Fernandina's government came the need for improvements in the dirt and oyster-shelled roads that ran through the island. This photograph depicts workers paving Centre Street. The original brick paving was continued to Atlantic Avenue, and that original brick is still in place under the asphalt.

Shipbuilding represented another important part of Fernandina's economy. This boat ws built in the first part of the 1900s on the north side of the entrance to Egan's Creek to catch menhaden. The natural curve of island oak trees made them excellent stock for building the hulls of large boats. (Courtesy P. K. Yonge Library of Florida History.)

Watercrafts were no strangers to Amelia. Large ships kept the island's many harbor pilots busy as they were constantly in port picking up lumber and other goods that were transported through Fernandina. This is an early postcard of the Fernandina waterfront. (Courtesy Florida State Archives.)

The trade taking place at Fernandina's port would not have been possible without the harbor's unique geographical features. The deep waters of the harbor, up to 60 feet, allowed large ships easy entry. This etching shows what the Fernandina harbor looked like on a typical day. The building across from the small bridge in the center of the etching is believed to be the island's first train depot. (Courtesy Florida State Archives.)

The intersection of the Amelia River's deep water and David Yulee's railroad are what led to the town's quick development and influx of capital during its Golden Age. This image shows the railroad tracks that ran parallel to the water for some distance down Front Street.

Much of what was shipped out of Fernandina had to do with the railroad itself. Cross ties were one of the primary goods shipped out of Fernandina's port. These cross ties were located at the docks owned by D. A. Cook.

Cotton was king in other parts of the South, but in Fernandina, lumber ruled. At any given time, tens of thousands of logs were stacked on the docks. The thick woods of the state's interior were cut down and hauled to Fernandina, where they were shipped off. In this photograph, barges are tied to the dock ready to float the stacks. A large pile driver is seen in the background.

With lumber in high demand, the port of Fernandina quickly grew into one of the leading ports in the country. As a result, many of the town's dignitaries, like Nathanial Borden, made a fortune shipping Florida oak and pine to ports all around the world. (Courtesy Florida State Archives.)

Large stacks of pine trees wait to be loaded on ships at the harbor. Logs like these were also moved by train across the state to Cedar Key, the western terminal of Yulee's railroad. From there, they might have been loaded on ships and delivered around the Gulf of Mexico. Here railcars loaded with lumber arrive between more stacks of cross ties.

Eventually larger steamships began to call on the port, competing with the schooners. Schooners of great size were still in operation though, and at one point, Fernandina's harbor was visited by the largest sailing ship in the world to pick up a load of lumber. At close inspection, horses are visible in this photograph as they were also an important part of port operations.

Lumber was not the only raw material coming through the port. Other resources from Florida's interior, like resin and phosphate, were also important exports. Barrels of resin line the docks before being loaded onto this large steamer. The flag on the bow of the ship is possibly the Mexican flag.

Bulky bales of marsh grass harvested from the areas around the island were also a common site on the docks. This product was used as mulch and insulation. Farmers also used the grass as inexpensive cattle feed, eliminating the need for salt licks and other supplements.

The high quality of Florida's lumber accounts, in part, for the economic success of Fernandina's port. It was the job of people like A. P. Murphy, pictured here with his wife, Nina, to properly inspect the lumber for quality.

There were many other people on the island whose livelihood depended on the business at the harbor. Scores of dockworkers, deckhands, and rail men like these were employed by the lumber agents, harbor pilots, and railroad company to see that the port ran in an efficient manner. John Cone is pictured on the far right. George Roux is to the left of him. The rest of the men are unidentified.

Besides the timber and marsh grass being harvested around town, there were other agricultural activities taking place on a smaller scale. This group of ducklings was kept in a Fernandina resident's backyard on the island.

These cows also lived on Amelia Island and would have provided milk and beef for their owners. They may have been purchased from the stock of cattle the Carnegies kept on nearby Cumberland Island.

Many of the island's farming operations were small-scale productions. Joseph Finnegan's 40-room home was located on the block bordered on the east and west by Eleventh and Twelfth Streets and on the north and south by Broome and Calhoun Streets. The home was among the islands most impressive and featured a large grove of orange and olive trees that Finnegan enjoyed. (Courtesy Florida State Archives.)

There were, however, larger farming operations on the island. These potatoes were grown by P. A. Goodbread. He grew the potatoes for the Nassau Truck and Farm Corporation on land that is presently home to the Smurfit-Stone Container paper mill.

The Ocean Breeze Farm was centrally located on the island near where the airport is today. This photograph captures a large and healthy celery crop, but many other crops were grown here as well.

Fishing was also a form of agriculture taking place off the docks. These sting rays were caught in the Amelia River and proudly displayed. Many islanders enjoyed frying their tender meat, which has a taste similar to calamari and scallops. Note the stacked lumber behind them. It seems lumber was inescapable along the docks during the 19th and early 20th centuries.

Fernandina's excellent fishing was so highly regarded it attracted some notable tourists. In 1932, lame-duck president Herbert Hoover spent part of his last Christmas holiday in office on Amelia Island. This picture was taken as President Hoover's boat headed out to fish from the local docks. Hoover is in the middle in the stern of the boat. He was well known as an avid fisherman.

Hoover was not the only president or dignitary to vacation in town, especially after the island reclaimed its reputation as a resort community in the 1970s. This is another picture of Hoover, this time aboard the presidential yacht the *Sequoia* as it left the island. Hoover mistakenly thought that a prominent display of his use of his recreational yacht would ease American spirit after the Depression.

Hoover's trip was not the first time the presidential yacht had docked at Fernandina. The above picture was taken as Frances Folsom Cleveland, wife of Grover Cleveland, was escorted back to the yacht after a short trip to Fernandina. Once on land, she was mobbed by local residents. Frankie, as she was known, was used to this kind of treatment as she enjoyed a celebrity status unusual for first ladies. The picture below further proves her celebrity status. It was taken of the crowd as they watched Mrs. Cleveland depart the island. Some people even climbed roofs to get a glimpse of her. Other political dignitaries to visit the island over the course of its history include Ulysses S. Grant, Robert E. Lee, George H. W. Bush, and Bill Clinton.

DUNGENESS,
CARNEGIE'S WINTER RESIDENCE,
11179 Fernandina, Fla.

The Carnegies, among the richest people in the world during the late 1800s, owned most of Cumberland Island. Cumberland lies just a few hundred yards north of Amelia across the state border and entrance to the Amelia River. The Carnegies built fabulous mansions on the otherwise undeveloped island. Since Cumberland was privately owned and lacked any commercial enterprises, its buildings were often erroneously credited to Fernandina. The photograph above did just that. It shows the Carnegie's 59-room mansion, known as Dungeness. It burned in 1959, but other Carnegie homes remain intact there. When the Carnegies came to town, they often used the boat in the lower photograph, the *Skibo*, to come to Fernandina.

Some of the less famous citizens of Fernandina used their own boats for leisure as well. This group enjoyed a fun day tooling around the island. They include, from left to right, one of the Bell twins (James or William), Marian Davis, and Henry Johnson.

Unfortunately, not all the time spent on boats offered so much enjoyment. Most of the boats in port were complicated vessels full of sails, engine parts, and equipment used to lift and transport heavy logs and barrels onboard. This photograph looks astern of one such ship docked at Fernandina.

It did not always take a celebrity to draw a crowd in Fernandina. Sometimes it just took some good weather. This postcard illustrates a busy summer day at the beach on Amelia. Days like this were not unusual, especially after the pavilion and casino were built.

Funerals were also capable of assembling a crowd on the island. This photograph was taken during the funeral of William Naylor Thompson at the First Presbyterian Church in September 1886. Thompson served in the House of Representatives and Senate. (Courtesy Florida State Archives.)

Camp Amelia
Copyrighted
by G.P.Freeman

CAMP

to by

One of the biggest crowds ever to assemble on early Amelia Island was in 1898 when the United States entered the Spanish-American War in an attempt to free Cuba from Spanish control. More than 10,000 volunteer soldiers were stationed at Fort Clinch as they awaited deployment to Cuba. The soldiers lived in tents, pictured here. The camp ran east from Tenth Street and

AMELIA,
1898.

BARTOV

north of Centre Street. It is worth noting that some of the rebellions that caused the war actually started in Fernandina. Cuban freedom fighter Jose Marti spent several months in Fernandina in 1894 planning a rebellion. He accomplished most of his work at the Florida House. The Spanish eventually caught wind of Marti's preparations and complained to the United States, who subsequently squashed the plan. Nevertheless, Marti's work on Amelia Island inspired many others in Cuba and eventually led to Cuba's independence. (Courtesy Florida State Archives.)

With the important role Amelia Island played throughout history as the buffer between Florida and the rest of the continental United States, the Spanish-American War was not the first time a large number of soldiers were stationed in Fernandina. This is an etching that depicts Union troops marching down North Second Street *c.* 1863. (Courtesy Florida State Archives.)

The Union may have occupied the island for most of the war, but most island residents were Confederates at heart. In 1907, Fernandina hosted a reunion for Confederate soldiers. Most of downtown was decorated, including this section of Centre Street between Third and Fourth Streets.

It was a common
practice for
troops garrisoned
in Fernandina to
parade through
the streets,
and many
civilians came
out to watch.
The troops
pictured here
were probably
part of the
group stationed
at Camp
Amelia during
the Spanish-
American War.
They march past
the Mularkey
brothers' store
and Frank
Simmon's
stationery
store here.

Parades have always been commonplace in Fernandina. This one took place in the early 1900s
and featured a car decorated with American flags followed by a brass band.

Holidays were always reason to celebrate in Fernandina. Central Park, designed by David Yulee, was the site of the local May Day festivities. This photograph, taken near the fountain that once graced the park, shows young girls dressed up as fairies. Marian Johnson enjoys the festivities from her baby carriage.

Christmas was another reason to celebrate, as was the case with this Christmas party for the employees at the Keystone Hotel.

The Christmas and winter season traditionally bring cold weather. Amelia Island may lie in Florida but it is not immune to low temperatures. This picture was taken after some chilly weather caused the fountain at the city waterworks to freeze over on January 25, 1905, a sight not often seen in Fernandina.

Sometimes, when conditions are just right, it snows in Fernandina. On extremely rare occasions, that snow sticks to the ground. Such was the case on this chilly day when snow accumulated on the roof of this island home in the early 1900s. In 1989, Fernandina received 1 inch of snow—an event that is still remembered locally as the "Blizzard of '89."

During more seasonable weather, island residents took their carts and bicycles right down to the beach. This photograph shows some of these in the background by the casino near what is presently known as Main Beach.

Technology would soon bring changes to the island. The first car in Fernandina was a chain-driven 1911 Buick owned by Dr. W. T. Waas. Bill Manchin, left, and John Lohman pose here with the car.

As more people on the island bought cars, they began taking them to the beach, and new opportunities became apparent. With 13 miles of flat sand, the beach became a perfect racetrack. Special cars like the one seen here were brought in to conduct races on the hard-packed sand.

What made the beach an ideal place to race cars also made it an ideal location for the island's first unofficial airport. From left to right, the beach cottages in the background belonged to the Haile, Brady, Weimer, and Rodgers families.

The Convent of the Sisters of St. Joseph was named in honor of some of Fernandina's most important women. In 1877, a yellow fever epidemic broke out in Fernandina. Local officials initially denied the outbreak, but as much as 70 percent of the local population fell ill. Grumblings of rioting began, and a National Guard unit was sent to assist. When quarantines finally were started, many people were sent to a small spit of land just across the Amelia River from the harbor known as Tiger Island. As a result, some people still refer to Tiger Island as Quarantine Island. Ultimately it was the Sisters of St. Joseph who took on the burden of caring for the sick and helped quell the problem. Four of the sisters caught the disease themselves, and two of those would eventually die from yellow fever, but not before averting the island from disaster. However, tragedy in Fernandina was unavoidable.

For all Fernandina had in its favor, it had a weakness that would play its part in bringing an end to the golden age. On March 23, 1876, flames broke out in a carpenter's shop near Centre Street. When the fire was extinguished, almost 40 buildings, essentially the island's entire business district, had been leveled. This photograph was taken the day after the fire as residents surveyed the damage. A few months after the fire, the city issued an ordinance that no wood frame structures could be built on Centre Street. However, this did not address structures on other streets. On September 6, 1883, a fire began at Streety's Tin Shop on North Second Street. That fire resulted in the burning of the entire block between Second and Third Streets along Centre Street. Those affected lost $40,000 worth of property, a substantial part of which was not insured. Both of these fires literally left their black mark on Fernandina's history and its economy.

This photograph was also taken after the 1876 fire but from a slightly different angle. From here, the Kydd building, which still stands today, is visible. It is worth noting that this building was the first brick building in Fernandina and the only on the north side of Centre Street that survived the fire. This fact, no doubt, had some influence on the ordinance that banned wooden buildings along Centre Street. The structure was built by brothers Thomas and James Kydd and housed a dry goods and fine clothing store. It was also home to the Kydd families. The town was blessed to have a dry goods store in operation after the fire. Most shop owners, however, began to rebuild immediately. Some even conducted business from their homes. (Courtesy Florida State Archives.)

St. Peter's Episcopal Church was also affected by fire on the morning of February 24, 1892. The cause was ruled as arson—perhaps the cause of the 1883 fire. R. M. Henderson had spent countless hours carving the lectern, baptismal font, and prayer desk out of curly pine, the extremely rare defected variety of wood that results in a unique pattern in the grain. When Henderson heard of the fire, he quickly made his way to the church and darted in and out of the flames to rescue his masterpieces. This feat nearly cost him his life when the floor collapsed beneath him. Nevertheless, his pieces were saved and they remain a part of the church's regular service. The original top of the church's tower, pictured above, was destroyed, however. The picture below was taken shortly after the fire and displays the exterior damage. The church was quickly restored, although Schuyler altered his original design of the tower and slightly changed the interior roof structure to accommodate the Harrison pipe organ.

The original casino on the beach eventually burned, too. This photograph was taken shortly after that fire. The building in the far background was the casino reserved for African Americans. The girl in the foreground is unidentified. The woman on the right is Mrs. Samuel Sayler with her dogs Ruby, Pearl, and Jack. The woman on the left was Mrs. Jack Mann, the wife of the fire captain.

The Burning of Phosphate Elevator
Fernandina Fla Aug 19-1907.

Another important part of the local economy went down in flames on August 19, 1907. The phosphate elevator, once the leading phosphate processing plant in the world, burned in spectacular fashion. It was partially rebuilt and continued to operate for a short time but never regained the prosperity it once knew.

118

Despite the costly damage and demoralizing nature of the fires the town experienced, they could not compare with what Mother Nature had in store. On September 28, 1898, the Weather Bureau West Indian reported a cyclonic storm had formed near Puerto Rico. Over the next few days, the storm strengthened and made its way along the Florida coast. At approximately 11:00 a.m. on October 2, the storm made landfall somewhere near Cumberland Island, just a few miles north of Fernandina. The National Weather Service has since combined data available from the day of the storm, personal accounts, and modern models to re-create the hurricane. These re-creations suggest the storm was likely a category four storm with maximum sustained winds of 135 miles per hour. This storm obviously caused intense damage to Amelia Island. Telegraph wires from St. Augustine to Savannah were destroyed. The ones seen here were located near downtown Fernandina.

This badly damaged photograph shows the destruction the hurricane caused to the docks. Unidentified Fernandina residents examine the damage and debris. The National Weather Service has since compared this storm to Hurricane Hugo, which struck Charleston in 1989.

The storm surge was estimated at 12 feet and water from the river encroached upon every building as far inland as Third Street. The offices of the local paper, the *Florida Mirror*, took water 4 feet deep. This storm's surge still holds most of the records in northeast Florida and southeast Georgia. This photograph shows the *Gladiator*, a tugboat used to assist the large ships coming in and out of port, beached along the destroyed docks. It was, perhaps, the best known boat in Fernandina. Some accounts have another ship washing several blocks inland.

Fittingly, this image shows the damage near David Yulee's house on the left. For all the work David Yulee did to put Fernandina on the map, the hurricane of 1898 was timed perfectly with Henry Flagler's railroad as the final nail in the coffin to take it off. The reports by some papers that Fernandina was "nearly destroyed" were not overestimated. The Strathmore Hotel and other beach structures were rubble. Most boats, so important to the locally economy, lay ruined in the marshes. All in all, the storm is still considered the worst storm ever to affect the island, as it caused $500,000 worth of damage to Fernandina, a tremendous amount at that time. David Yulee's railroad, once the cradle of the town's prosperity, faced another critical setback as miles of track were torn from their foundation. Yulee, having passed away years earlier, could no longer provide his exceptional leadership to aid in the recovery, nor could the other residents recover from too many financial losses from fire and disaster compounded by a waning economy thanks to Flagler's railroad. Fernandina's golden age had come to an end.

After some less hopeful times, the industry on the island was able to rebound. The paper mills played a key part in the revitalization of the island, providing hundreds of jobs to residents. They stabilized the economy and paved the way for future development and recovery. This photograph was taken on October 31, 1937, from the well tower and shows what would become the digester and screen buildings for the Rayonier mill.

The early parts of the 20th century represent some of the bleakest times Fernandina and Amelia Island had seen. Problems grew worse during the Depression of the 1930s. Some of the vacant land in this picture soon helped change the situation. The land in the foreground is the property that would eventually become the Rayonier mill. Farther upstream, the area that became the Smurfit-Stone Container mill is visible. This is one of the last photographs that includes the boardwalk across the marsh. It shows the rest of downtown Fernandina shortly before it entered a new era of prosperity.

The Nassau Fertilizer Company, or pogie plant, also created jobs that were important to Fernandina's recovery. The plant processed a small, local fish known as pogie into fertilizer. As can be imagined, the plant produced an extremely foul odor that engulfed the island on days when the wind blew in the wrong direction.

These men are pursuing a school of pogie, also known as menhaden, and have placed a large net in the water just off Amelia Island. Once the pogie were in the net, a winch was used to haul them onboard. The fish were then taken to the processing plant where rich oil was extracted from their bodies. The oil was used mainly as fertilizer but was also used in cosmetics, paints, inks, and pet food.

The shrimping industry also contributed to Fernandina's resurgent economy. The island is known as the birthplace of the modern shrimping industry thanks in large part to the efforts of Fernandina shrimpers like William Corkum, pictured here. Corkum invented a device called the otter trawl, which made dragging the ocean bottom for shrimp a simpler process. The otter trawl is still in use today.

Fleet of Shrimp Boats and Packing House, Fernandina, Fla.

After William Jones Davis first used a power-driven boat to shrimp deeper waters, Fernandina flourished as a shrimping community. The docks the lumber ships had deserted were repopulated with shrimp boats like the ones shown here. A shrimp processing facility was also constructed. (Courtesy Florida State Archives.)

Shrimping became increasingly central to Amelia Island's 20th-century recovery as business opportunities like net production arose. In 1963, the island held its First Annual Shrimp Festival, which featured shrimp boat races and other festivities. The festival is still held every year during the first weekend in May and now brings over 200,000 people to the island each year.

Tourism would also return to the island as luxury resorts and homes filled the south end of the island in the 1980s. To welcome Amelia's visitors by boat, this structure was built at the foot of the Centre Street docks. When the city redesigned the waterfront in the 1970s, this building was dropped into the ocean to serve as an artificial reef.

Nearly 100 years after the island's golden age began, downtown Fernandina had seen many changes. This photograph, taken in 1963 at the base of the docks, looks east towards the beach. It was taken very near the same location as the photograph on page nine and nearly 100 years later.

BIBLIOGRAPHY

Amelia Island: Isle of Eight Flags. DVD. Fernandina Beach, FL: Pirate Television, 2007.

Amelia Island Museum of History. "Docent Training Manual." November 2004.

www.fairbankshouse.com/history.html.

"Fire Destroys Downtown Business Block." *Florida Mirror*. September 6, 1883.

Garriott, E. B. "Forecasts and Warnings." *Monthly Weather Review* 26. No. 10 (1898).

Johannes, Jan H. *Yesterday's Reflections II: Nassau County, Florida*. Fernandina Beach, FL: Lexington Ventures, 2000.

Hardee, Suzanne Davis. *The Golden Age of Amelia Island: A Glimpse*. Fernandina Beach, FL: Amelia Island Museum of History, 1993.

goflorida.about.com/od/ameliaisland/ss/ameliaisland_4.htm

www.lighthousefriends.com/light.asp?ID=346

Litrico, Helen Gordon. "The Bell Houses." *Amelia Now* (1983).

———. "Jose Marti and the Fernandina Filibuster." *Amelia Now* (1989).

stpetersparish.org/about-us/history

www.sequoiayacht.com/index.cfm?content=45

Visit us at
arcadiapublishing.com

CPSIA information can be obtained
at www.ICGtesting.com
Printed in the USA
BVHW011524041021
618093BV00004B/375

9 781531 633035